HOW TO TALK TO PEOPLE:

Having a better conversation, improve social skills, master small talk and build meaningful relationship.

Samuel Gomez

All rights reserved.No part of this publication may be reproduced, distributed, or transmitted in any form or by any means, including photocopying, recording or other electronic or mechanical methods, without the prior written permission of the publisher, except in the case of brief quotations embodied in critical reviews and certain other noncommercial uses permitted by copyright law.copyright © Samuel Gomez, 2022.

Table of contents

Chapter 1 Struggling on how to talk to people

Chapter 2 How to start a conversation with people

Chapter 3 Master small talk

Chapter 4 Becoming a better listener when talking to people and to interact with new people.

Chapter 1 Struggling on how to talk to people

Hard To Talk? Reasons Why And What To Do About It

Lots of us get self-conscious or apprehensive during talks, which might mean that we struggle to express ourselves effectively. This makes interactions incredibly tough and might even leave you feeling silent.

1. Trying to talk too rapidly

Trying to speak too rapidly might make it hard to converse in lots of different ways. You could trip over your words, talk too rapidly for other people to comprehend, and occasionally you might find yourself expressing something you didn't intend to say.

Give yourself time

Allowing yourself to talk more slowly makes it less likely that you'll make any of those faults. Try taking a breath before you start speaking rather than rushing directly into the discussion. Use this time to make sure that you know what you're going to say before you start speaking.

It could also assist to attempt to talk more slowly when you're speaking. Public speaking gurus encourage individuals to talk more slowly than seems natural, and that's true for many of us in discussions as well. It might be good to practice this in the mirror or chat with yourself while you're at home alone.

2. Making too many "filler" noises

Lots of us find ourselves repeating "umm," "uh," or "like" over and over again as we strive to find the exact thing to express, and these may be useful. They do need to be in moderation, however. If you use them too often, you can seem less convincing, or you might feel upset with yourself that you can't simply "get to the point."

Practice stating things plainly

This is something I've battled with a lot, and writing for a living has helped. It's pushed me to explain things honestly and simply. I used to attempt to bring too many concepts together in big, convoluted words. That meant that I would frequently need to think out how best to explain myself as I was already speaking. I would instinctively "cover" such times with a filler sound, like "umm."

Try putting your ideas down or recording yourself speaking. Think about the sentences you've used and if you might have phrased them more clearly. For example, I may say:"Yesterday, I was chatting with Laura, my dog walker, about whether we should work on recall or if it would be better to enhance the way that Oak pays attention to me while we're on walks first."

Honestly, you may have to read it a couple of times to make sense of it. It would be easier if I said:

"I was chatting to Laura, my dog walker, yesterday. We wanted to make Oak more mannered on walks, and we came up with two choices. The first is to concentrate exclusively on recall. The alternative is to focus on having him pay attention to me during walks first, and then we can work on recall later."

This was simpler to follow, and I would be less inclined to add filler words since I wouldn't have to think about how to end the phrase. Sounding more authoritative and being simpler to comprehend will both enhance your communication.

If you do find yourself unable to think of what to say next, attempt to stop rather than use a filler phrase. You may not even realize when you use them, so try asking a buddy to bring them out to you.

3. Finding it tough to communicate about emotions

Lots of individuals find it simple to speak about facts or current events but struggle to talk about their emotions or how something is affecting them. This can be because you don't want to make anybody else feel uncomfortable, or you might be terrified of rejection.

Not wanting to communicate our sentiments frequently comes down to a lack of confidence in the individuals we're talking to. We may not trust them to care about us or to be attentive and compassionate when we're feeling vulnerable.

Develop trust steadily

Building trust is seldom simple, and it's crucial not to hurry it. Trying to push yourself to trust someone too readily might lead to you trusting someone more than they deserve and things going wrong as a consequence.

Instead, attempt to provide faith in little amounts. You don't need to speak about your darkest, most terrible emotions immediately away. Try expressing a preference, such as "I adore that band" or even "That film made me incredibly sad."

Notice how much other individuals share with you. You'll probably discover that other individuals will start to talk more about their sentiments the more you share yours. Only disclose as much as you feel secure revealing, but try to push a bit towards the borders of your comfort zone.

4. Struggling to find words

That sensation when the appropriate phrase is "on the tip of your tongue" is tremendously aggravating and may quickly derail your discussion. It occurs more commonly with nouns and names than it does with other words. Almost everyone battles with tip-of-the-tongue events relatively often (approximately once a week),[1] but it may leave you feeling uneasy and humiliated.

Be honest

Trying to disguise the fact that you've forgotten a term, or pressing yourself to recover it soon, can frequently make it worse. Being honest about the fact that you've forgotten the term and how it makes you feel may help.

Take this survey and receive a bespoke report based on your unique personality and objectives. Start boosting your confidence, your communication skills, or your capacity to connect - in less than an hour.

Start the quiz.

Recently, I was a little anxious, and I realized that I was trying to find the correct word a lot. I attempted to hide it, saying "thingy" or "wotsit" if I couldn't recall. My boyfriend thought this incredibly humorous and laughed at me, which made me feel worse. He wasn't trying to be cruel. He simply didn't realize that I was feeling awful.

After a week or two, I explained. I added, "I know you're not trying to be nasty, but I'm struggling to find the proper words at the moment. I don't like it, and it makes me feel horrible when you laugh at me about it.

He stopped calling attention to it. I stopped saying "thingy." Instead, I stopped speaking when I couldn't find the proper term. I'd answer, "Nope. I can't recall the word," and we'd work together to hash it out. After only a few days, it had stopped happening so regularly.

Try being honest when you can't find the words. Because everyone understands how it feels to have a word on the tip of your tongue, most people will want to assist you to find the perfect term as soon as they notice. Being able to say that you're suffering may also help you appear more confident to others and even make you feel more confident yourself, which is an additional plus.

5. Not being able to express ideas

Sometimes the difficulty isn't that you're trying to find certain words, but rather that you can't find a method to put your ideas into words at all. You could instantly "know" what you want to say but not be able to describe it in a manner that makes sense to others.

Sometimes, you know you're not expressing yourself effectively, and other times you believe what you've said is obvious, but the other person doesn't "get it." This may make talks incredibly difficult and leave you feeling alienated.

Get your ideas clearly in your head first
Most of the time, we're a lot better at communicating things when we grasp the issue fully. When we "kinda know" what we're attempting to express, we might get muddled and confused. This then confuses anybody we're talking to. Take a minute before you speak to be clear about what you're trying to express. If you're attempting to explain something particularly sophisticated and you're scared thinking it through would take too long, you may even say so.

6. Being too weary to focus on discussion
Being weary or sleep-deprived may make communication exceedingly tough. The more exhausted I am, the more I say the incorrect thing, mumble, and (sometimes) spew total nonsense. You may notice the difference if you've remained up all night, but a longer-term lack of sleep can lead to subtle issues in making conversation.

Rest and avoid crucial chats while you're asleep
We all know that it's vital to get enough sleep, but this may be tough, particularly in a busy contemporary world or when you're highly worried. Keeping proper sleep hygiene is key.

It's also beneficial to self-monitor and attempt to notice when you're not at your best due to a lack of sleep. If you recognize that you're weary (and probably a bit irritable too), attempt to postpone essential interactions until a time when you're better prepared to cope with them.

7. Becoming tongue-tied talking to a crush

No matter how fluent or confident you are, chatting with someone you're romantically interested in may increase the stakes of the discussion and make it much more difficult. For most of us, this might then drive us to struggle to express ourselves, panic and say something dumb or withdraw into our shells and keep silent. None of these is a very useful reaction when you're with the guy or woman of your dreams.

When we look at someone from a distance, we construct a picture in our head as to what type of a person they are. Try to remember that this is your picture of them, not the person. Until you get to know someone, you're essentially being drawn to your idea of them.

Lower the stakes of the discussion

Talking to your crush doesn't have to be about sweeping them off their feet or astonishing them with your intellect and wit. The idea is to show them, honestly, who you are and to attempt to find out who they are. Try telling yourself, "This isn't a seduction. I'm attempting to get to know this person."

It may also be useful to have more frequent, shorter chats. If you believe that a discussion is your only opportunity to impress someone, you're more likely to be concerned about it than if it's simply one chat among many. This might assist you to relax and be yourself.

8. Zoning out

Almost everyone understands what it feels like to zone out during a discussion. Zoning out is terrible enough, but it may be exceedingly tough to resume the discussion after your focus has come back. This is

because you could not completely comprehend what others are talking about now or be apprehensive about repeating what someone else has stated earlier.
Improve your attention
In this scenario, prevention is better than treatment. We have tons of recommendations to assist you to prevent zoning out in the first place, so try to practice at least a few of them.

If you want to enhance your social skills, self-confidence, and capacity to connect with someone, you may take our 1-minute questionnaire.
Start the quiz.
If you find you have zoned out, the greatest approach might sometimes be to apologize and then refresh your focus. As long as you don't do this too frequently, most people will understand and be thankful for your honesty.

9. Avoiding uncomfortable subjects
Sometimes we're completely comfortable establishing talks about broad subjects, but we struggle to speak about unpleasant difficulties that we're now facing. Not being able to communicate present sorrow may leave us feeling alienated, vulnerable, and prone to depression and self-harm. [2]\sAsk for what you need
When things are extremely challenging, it's perfectly OK to ask for precisely what you need. Most people will be pleased that you've provided them with a handbook, since they may be concerned about how to aid you.

Often, this might include them simply sitting with you, without expecting you to chat. If that's what you need, try expressing, "I really can't speak about this right now, but I don't want to be alone. Would you simply sit with me for a while?"

You may discover that you want to chat about things after a time of sitting together, or you may not. Whatever you need is OK.

10. Feeling that conversing isn't worth the effort
Sometimes you might struggle to speak to others because it seems like much more work than you're ready to pay. I believe most individuals can sympathize with that experience.

There are two aspects to this issue. One is that chatting with other people may require a lot of energy. The other is that chatting to people might seem unrewarding. Either of these might lead to you believing that making conversation simply isn't worth the effort.

If there are only a few individuals that leave you feeling this way, try to recognize that the fault may not lay with you. It may not be their fault either. It's simply that the two of you don't gel well together. If you feel this way about most or all individuals, you may want to think about your underlying beliefs.

Prioritize your emotions to decrease tiredness
It may surprise you to realize that plenty of socially talented individuals find talking to people quite tiresome. This is because we're attempting to read the other person's body language, grasp their position, think about the discussion subject, and think about what we're

going to say, all at the same time. That's a lot to think about, and we have our sentiments to handle as well.

If you're avoiding talking to people because of the hard effort required in paying attention to their sentiments, consider permitting yourself to concentrate more on yourself than on the other person.
Try stating to yourself, "I'm not responsible for them. My responsibility is to make sure that I enjoy this conversation." I'm not advocating that you be a jerk, but you don't need to be so aware of the other person's wants that it's putting you on edge.
Understand the aim of small chat to find it enjoyable
Small chat is seldom gratifying in and of itself, particularly if you're more introverted than outgoing. Try to adjust your thinking and perceive small chat as being about creating connections and trust. During unrewarding interactions, try reminding yourself:\s"I may not care about the weather/traffic/celebrity gossip, but I'm proving that I can be trusted. This is how I acquire deeper talks and friendships."

11. Mental health concerns
Many distinct mental health conditions are related to trouble making conversation or failing to enjoy such talks. Social anxiety, depression, Aspergers, and ADHD are well renowned for their influence on your communication, as well as more specialized illnesses like as selective mutism.
Seek therapy for underlying disorders

For other individuals, a diagnosis might seem like a definitive judgment, imposing boundaries on their social interactions forever. For others, it might seem like an opportunity, to allow them access to the aid and therapy they need to better their life.

Try to remember that you don't need to suffer in quiet. Seek therapy with a practitioner you trust. Your doctor will normally be your first port of contact, but don't be hesitant to choose someone who makes you feel comfortable.

6 Types of People Who Are Hard to Talk To:

Certain individuals are adept at feeding their egos. If you've ever been trapped by a particularly insecure or competitive personality in the work arena, you know how uncomfortable these sorts of encounters can be.

They make discussion seem like a type of torment — yet it's possible to negotiate even the hardest encounters with elegance.

1. The braggart. This dialogue-destroyer stresses status and riches. He'll reveal how much money he earns, with the topic continuously centered around his spanking new Ferrari or his Fifth Avenue condo.

Often, the not-so-humblebrags are conveyed indirectly. He'll tell you how the insurance on his boat has tripled in the last year, or how he wishes his girlfriend would stop purchasing Birkin bags. Whenever you run with a braggart, recognize his good fortune and then change the conversation.

2. The rumormonger. This individual is constantly at the center of rumor and turmoil. She'll immerse herself in everyone else's personal life and make it her business to disseminate delicious gossip.

Whenever you stumble across a rumormonger, change the topic — or better yet, excuse yourself. Most essential, never disclose anything confidential with her. If she's spreading other people's personal business around, you can guarantee she'll do the same thing with yours.

3. The one-upper. This person will let you know that, whatever you've done, he's got a story to top it. "Oh, you just got back from scaling Mount Kilimanjaro? That's a terrific beginner's trip. Climbing Everest was one of the most fulfilling experiences of my life."

The one-upper loves to feel significant. It might be a hardship — but be patient and ask questions. "It's fantastic to meet a fellow mountain climber. What was the toughest element of your Everest trip?"

4. The hard-hearted. This person has no filter. She expresses whatever's on her mind with little care for others' sentiments. Typically, this individual isn't purposely nasty, but she cannot communicate herself without it being seen as unpleasant or impolite. "You're looking incredibly thin. Have a chocolate brownie. You could stand to add a few pounds."

Avoid the impulse to reply defensively. The easiest method to handle this issue is to kill her with kindness or deflect the statement with comedy or charm. "Thank you for your concern. I'm attempting to reduce a few pounds so I can look as nice as you!"

5. The brain-picker. This guy takes and never gives back. He'll corner you and ask countless questions, constantly searching for free advice. "You're a dermatologist? Will you look at this mole on my arm? Should I be concerned?" Don't distribute your precious information for free. Respond with something like, "Call my office first thing Monday morning and my assistant will make an appointment for you."

6. The rambler. We've all had the experience of being held captive by a rambler at a networking event. This individual speaks at you instead of with you. She believes she's being sociable by chatting, but monopolizes the discussion and shows all the signs of a chronic non-listener — constantly interrupting.
Try to introduce the rambler to someone else or excuse yourself gracefully. Make sure to engage and remain in charge of the discussion, though, before you withdraw.

Chapter 2 How to start a conversation with people

Tips On How To Start a Conversation
1. Keep It Pleasant: Your talk should begin in a positive tone. Avoid venting your feelings or voicing unpleasant comments. You can always find something good to say, regardless matter how horrible things are.
Remark subjects like the weather, the food, the people you're with, or the event entirely. It's a fantastic technique to start a topic by stating something simple like "I'm having a lovely time" and anticipating that the person you wish to chat with is having a good time as well. Even if the scenario isn't perfect, try to find the good side of things.
A favorable comment is more likely to generate a favorable reaction than a negative one. It indicates that you are a nice person who is aware of what is going on. Keeping a cheerful attitude also helps individuals relax. People will be more interested in having a chat with you as a reward.

2. Start Simple: A deep, philosophic, earth-shattering statement isn't necessary to start every fantastic discussion. Simple initial words or inquiries are a terrific way to get the discussion started.

It may sound trite to make remarks about the weather, the locale, or the food, but there's a reason why this style of introduction works so successfully. It's a fundamental, uncomplicated approach to start a dialogue by giving some basis point between two persons. Talking about minor stuff may lead to deeper talks about individual ideas, backgrounds, hobbies, and other concerns that could help individuals build social bonds.

3. Ask For Help: A better strategy to start a debate is to ask a question. This provides you a reason to engage with the other individual as well as enables them to aid you. While employing this method, begin with something uncomplicated that can be accomplished with little effort. For instance, you may query about the start time of a seminar or routes to a given place.
Asking a fundamental inquiry could lead to an extra debate about other subjects, which is one of the benefits of this strategy. Even after you've posed your query and the other person has promised to assist, you and your conversation partner have made a type of mutual alliance. It's now up to you to show your appreciation and identify yourself since they've supplied their help. This is a fantastic time for both of you to get to know each other better

4. Body Language: What we don't communicate is frequently just as significant as what you do. It's vital to pay attention to your nonverbal cues when beginning a fresh topic. Interest and enthusiasm may be shown by body language.

A nice smile, a comfortable attitude, and establishing eye contact, for one, could suggest that you want to learn more about this other person. Slouching, looking away, and frowning may create the appearance that you are annoyed or disinterested in the talks.

5. Listen And Expressing Interest: Trying to converse with someone with whom you don't appear to have much in common could be daunting. Engaging the other person to speak about their interests, work, or abilities is a smart technique to start a dialogue in such contexts.

Ask inquiries like what the other person loves doing, then pay attention to what they reply. Everyone loves discussing their hobbies, therefore demonstrating a genuine interest in what other people value may be a terrific conversation starter.

6. Strike A Balance: There is no "one-size-fits-all" technique for having a good dialogue. The greatest conversations mix asking questions, listening to what others have to say, and sharing personal information. Asking open-ended questions that cannot be answered with a simple "yes" or "no" may also be effective. Instead of asking, "Did you enjoy the speaker?" you may enquire, "How did you like the speaker?"

Learning how to begin a conversation is a crucial talent that may help you build social ties in different settings. It may be tricky at first, particularly if you suffer from shyness or social anxiety, but practice is the key to becoming more at ease speaking with people. Consider these trades to be a trial run. Your communication talents will increase as you start interacting with people more regularly.

7. Avoid Conversation Killers: Although it typically isn't emphasized enough, there are many topics you should avoid addressing until you are extremely comfortable with the people you are chatting with.
While your family may launch talks with opinion articles, gossip, critiques, and inappropriate jokes during reunions, this is often not a great conversation starter. There are other proper moments for sharing your views or even trying to persuade someone but be assured such concerns are acceptable before engaging in a heated conversation.
When it comes to starting up a conversation with a stranger, it is advisable to follow the safe approach. This conversation opener is less daunting, but it still challenges the other person to react in some manner.

8. Be Funny: This doesn't imply you have to perform a stand-up act; crack a few jokes and tell them a fantastic yarn to get the discussion started. You'll be shocked at how sharing entertaining anecdotes may motivate others to reveal their sentiments. Everyone likes laughing, and laughing makes others feel at ease. This is a wonderful approach to loosen up those tense folks and get them conversing.
To catch the person's attention, utilize your wit. Demonstrate that you're a rapid thinker who appreciates wordplay, funny jokes, and general chat. Use it if you have a terrific amusing narrative, as long as it's not too

lengthy. If you tell a lengthy tale that you haven't tried before, it may not earn you the reaction you hoped.

9. Have more discussions with individuals you don't know: The probability that you'll have a nice conversation grows with the quantity you have. You grow more competent at presenting better inquiries and offering more intelligent responses. Although there is some expertise, confidence comes more from just doing it more regularly. We fear that the other person won't accept us or won't give us any attention because of social anxiety.
Contrary to common opinion, research suggests that most individuals are ready to initiate a conversation when invited to do so by another person. The societal standards of politeness are not taken into consideration in our ideas about fear.

10. Learn to pick up visual queues: There are occasions when folks will have objects on them that might betray some of their interests. Keep an eye out for them, and when you find one, utilize it as a springboard for dialogue.
You can discover out about someone's interests in literature and music by noting if they are carrying a book in their hand or wearing huge headphones around their neck, but not while they are actively reading or listening. T-shirts featuring logos or movie and television memorabilia are also good discussion starters, especially if you are a fan.

For both physical and emotional health, it is crucial to maintain strong social bonds. Forming social relationships has been associated with better immune function, increased longevity, reduced anxiety levels, more empathy for others, and higher self-esteem, according to research. You'll be better able to develop the social ties that are so crucial to your health and well-being if you master the skill of initiating a conversation.

Ways to start a discussion with people and their examples
In the workplace, you may use a range of themes to start a discussion as long as they are acceptable for the context. Conversations with coworkers or professional connections will be different from those with new friends or acquaintances. Your early attempts might spark a dialogue that may pay off by helping you create important connections with coworkers and colleagues. Here are some discussion starters for the workplace:

1. Ask for information
An excellent technique to start a discussion is to ask for information from the person you want to speak to. This is a good, natural technique to create rapport with someone fast. Even if you already know the answer, it is still an excellent technique to approach someone if you cannot think of another subject.
For example, if you are attending an event and encounter a colleague you have not chatted to yet, you might question them about the conference.

Example: "Do you know whether the regional director will speak after the opening session?"

With this, you may extend the discussion even further by noting something you admire about the speakers and so on.

2. Pay a compliment
Complimenting someone may brighten their day and enhance their confidence. You may choose anything about the person you like and say why you like it.

Example: "I truly like your hair. The cut fits you."

There are various follow-up questions you may ask to keep the discussion going such as where they go to have their hair trimmed or how they choose the style.

3. Comment on something nice
You can typically find something nice to say about an event or scenario. The occasion may have been the final workplace happy hour or a sports event that was on the night before. If the individual shares your beliefs, you are on your way to a stimulating discussion.

Example: "Did you see the football game last night? I believe our squad finally reached its stride."

From then, the talk may continue further into the game or a tangential issue such as a different sports team.

23

4. Introduce yourself

While this may not be suited for every scenario, introducing oneself is a clear approach to conveying your interest in meeting someone. If you recently began a new job and have not met someone in another department yet, you may approach them and introduce yourself.

Example: "Hi, I'm Lisa. I'm new to the team and wanted to introduce myself."

You may then ask follow-up inquiries about their job or how long they have been with the organization.

Related: How To Introduce Yourself in an Interview\s5. Offer aid

If you find yourself in a position to aid someone you want to speak to, grasp the situation and assist them. Offering aid may make you popular and acquire the confidence of the other person, particularly when you show real care.

Example: "Can I help you file away some of those binders?" or "Do you need a seat?"

From there, you may lead into a talk relevant to the assignment such as what is in the contents of the binders.

6. Ask for assistance

Requesting aid is another good conversation opener. It works because it helps the other person feel useful, particularly if it's something they can offer readily. If someone performs you a favor, they may be more inclined to think of you in a good way and trust you. Asking for assistance might help you start a polite discussion but make sure your request is convenient for the other person.

Example: "Could you tell me where this conference room is located?" or "Could I borrow a pen from you?"

7. Mention a shared experience
If you want to chat with someone who you know has something in common with you, you can always pick a subject as a conversation point. Your shared experiences make getting along easier and that facilitates the flow of the discussion and the formation of the friendship.

Example: "When was the last time you saw our buddy Rachel?" or "How do you appreciate working in the Philly office?"

8. Ask an opinion
Soliciting other people's views indicates you appreciate and are interested in what they have to say. If they are knowledgeable about the issue, many individuals will eagerly answer your inquiries and get a discussion started. When asking for an opinion, consider issues relevant to the present.

Example: "How do you enjoy the coffee from the new cafe?" or "Are they (name brand) shoes? Are they comfortable?"

9. Praise the individual
When you meet an executive or notable person in your business for the first time, a nice method to start a discussion is to compliment their work.

Example: "I heard the speech you delivered at the banquet last week. You made some pretty solid points."

Follow up the praise with questions pertinent to the compliment such as how they become such a brilliant public speaker.

10. Show real curiosity
See if you can locate a subject you know the individual is enthusiastic about. Passions may get your colleagues chatting and you can learn something new. Remember to keep the dialogue polite and encouraging.

Example: "I notice your T-shirt reads [band name]. Have you gone to one of their shows?" or "I read on the welcome email that you recently relocated here from Barbados. What is it like there?"

11. Ask about them
People naturally appreciate talking about themselves. Try choosing a subject that will enable the individual to talk about their hobbies, family, or experiences.

Example: "That's a lovely picture of your family on your desk. How old are your children?" or "I heard that you just took vacation time to visit Hawaii, how was it?"

12. Make an observation
The place you're in may provide several discussion starters. Commenting about the structure, temperature or artwork may all be fantastic ways to start a person chatting with you.

Example: "They did a terrific job decorating this office" or "The views from this window are beautiful!"

13. Comment on the weather
If everything else fails, you can always remark about the weather. It is one of the simplest methods to start someone chatting and can flow into several other subjects.

Example: "It's a gorgeous day, isn't it?" or "Can you believe all the snow we're getting?"

Family
You may ask queries concerning relationships, siblings, children, or even pets. So long as your communication skills are adequate and the inquiries are not too private, individuals will typically feel happy to share openly about their relatives.

This is a wonderful subject for a company happy hour or a team event. It is a strategy to engage in small chats and learn more about a person fast.

Example: "What sort of dog do you have?"

Sports
People are enthusiastic about sports and will happily express their excitement. You may ask inquiries about their favorite teams, tournaments, and athletic events.

Example: "Did you watch the penalty kick the U.S. had against Portugal?"

Entertainment
In the era of on-demand entertainment and blockbuster TV programs, entertainment is an essential conversation subject for many individuals. If you ask someone about their favorite TV program or series, the odds are that they will have one or two they watch.

Example: "Have you seen the newest superhero movie?" or "Did you see the music awards event last night?"

News
Being updated on the latest news might help you initiate small chats effortlessly with strangers and acquaintances. Whether you are a lover of conventional newspapers or follow digital alternative news sources, you can always initiate a dialogue with questions about local news, occurrences in other regions of the globe,

and others. However, it is often preferable to keep political news out of the workplace.

Example: "Did you hear about that hero dog that rescued a youngster from a fire?"

Work
Many individuals take delight in talking about their employment and will readily offer ideas on the part they play in the business. Whether you are chatting to a person in your organization or someone you met lately, asking inquiries about their tasks at work will certainly generate a response.

Example: "How do you enjoy handling escrow accounts?"

Chapter 3 Master small talk

Small chats are something most people dislike, however when done well, it's a fantastic opportunity to get to know people and generate a welcoming environment. Moreover, it's only a warm-up before you delve into actual interactions.

But if you're not a social butterfly, I can think it might be scary.

If it makes you feel any better, I used to be completely bad at it, and it concerned me since, without it, it's impossible to develop new acquaintances and relationships. I began exercising it, and soon I was able to talk to anybody without any anxiety and more importantly, without them or myself feeling uncomfortable.

Here are some recommendations on how you may enhance your small chat abilities yourself.

1) PRACTICE SMALL TALKS EVERYWHERE

Let's face it, you can't improve without practice. Being excellent at small chats is a blend of being able to begin discussions to keeping good conversations going.

Leaving the practice for real networking events and parties is like not practicing boxing until you reach the ring. I believe we both agree that that would be ridiculous.

Small discussions are no different.

If you truly want to improve, do what I used to do when I worked on developing it. I had a goal to begin several little discussions a day. You may start with 1 and progressively raise the number to 10. It may sound like a huge amount, but it isn't. Look, to progress, you need to push yourself a little.

I chatted to folks at work, the store assistant, and cashiers, I messaged or contacted my friends or individuals I had not spoken to for a long. Not only this will greatly expedite your growth, but you'll also increase your friendships.

The dialogue might be brief. A few casual phrases are an excellent start.

It's a trivial conversation, not a "deep and meaningful."

2) STOP TRYING TO BE INTERESTING, BUT RATHER BE INTERESTED

Many individuals experience a big strain when it comes to small chats because they feel like they have to be incredibly engaging and amusing.

Yet, the greatest way to end a discussion is to make it all about yourself.

Think about it. A stranger walks up and begins chatting to you about himself. You'd be like "Ermmm, I didn't ask."

But, if you want to persuade the individual to participate in a discussion, be inquisitive, ask them suitable questions, shut talking and listen.

3) ASK THE RIGHT QUESTIONS

The greatest questions are the ones that are related to what's going around. I call the situational questions. Just glance around and ask anything that makes sense.
"How do you know "the name" (the host, the person who's celebrating, the performer, etc.)?
It might be an inquiry concerning the area, the event, or something that occurred before or will happen.
A fantastic technique to start a discussion is to compliment something about the individual and then ask them about it.
Keep it light and Keep it relatable.

4) BUILD ON OR BRANCH OUT OF THE SMALL TALK
When you touch on a subject, think about what would be the next logical inquiry that is pertinent to the previous issue. Where may the discussion branch off?
If you're at a birthday garden party and you inquired about how the individual knows the birthday girl, and they stated it's via work, you might then ask:\s– about what they do.
– how long they've been friends.\s– how they met.
– whether they've gone to previous garden parties.\s– if they are making the most of the summer.
The options are unlimited, but they are all something tied to what you've just spoken about.
Being genuinely inquisitive while without being invasive is the ideal strategy.
People have fantastic tales and know intriguing stuff.
Tap into it, and they will do all the talking, and you will truly appear like someone who is genuinely engaged.
Just regard it as getting to know someone.

5) SMALL TALK TOPICS TO AVOID

Certain things are simply best to ignore initially since it generally entirely alienates the dialogue. I've been on both sides of it.

A) Talking about contentious themes. With issues like politics, religion, war, and anything similar where you can anticipate strong polarity (and less understanding) you're entering into the risky region of deepening the gaps between you two or even initiating an argument. That's not going to help. This is not the moment for you to be correct or preach what's right.

B) Giving guidance. Occasionally you'll chat with someone who has something on their chest and will share with you more about what they are going through. As tempting as it may be, refuse to be a smart ass and start offering them advice (particularly if you're a coach. We are very guilty of this). Nothing wrong with you trying to assist. But initially, you don't know whether the individual is ready. Secondly, it's most likely, not the ideal moment and setting for it.

C) Deep Topics. Save your deep and significant convos for your discussion group or your buddies. I have been in circumstances where I was at a party and people began to speak to me about death, extraterrestrial life, conspiracy theories, consciousness, etc. I enjoy all those things, but not when I'm trying to have a good time. If someone says "Okayyyy, I'm going to join my pals now." You've probably gone too deep.

6) IF THE SMALL TALK IS PAINFUL, LEAVE
Sometimes, small discussions don't go well even when you're trying your best.

It may not be your fault. Sometimes folks are simply not interested or are plain dull or antisocial, or who knows. Don't feel forced to wrestle with them. Give it a solid go, and if you perceive a lack of interest, turn away.

Just say, "Okayyyy, nice speaking with you, I'm going to join my pals now. See you around."

You don't need to explain anything. You're not there to amuse anybody. If they are not up for it, leave them alone.

The following is a fantastic start for you to start your small chat skill.

If you are seeking a magic phrase that will make you appear entertaining and will convert you into a social butterfly, there is no such thing. Small chat is a talent that may easily be learned. It only requires a little practice. If you're shying away from it, my "from the heart advice" is - to grow a pair! It's merely a small conversation. The worst thing that can happen is that people won't converse much. Big deal.

Steps on perfecting the art of small chat
Inform yourself every day.
Put a question mark on it.

Look for Showing genuine interest in the other person by asking questions and listening is crucial.

Though typically thought of as insignificant and surface-level, small chats may be critical when it comes to developing connections and relationships. In the field of business in especially, the gift of small chat may considerably increase an entrepreneur's networking chances, potentially even resulting in new transactions, partnerships, or vendor connections.

But understanding how to create small conversation doesn't always come effortlessly, and utilizing small talk to your advantage to build relationships and establish vital connections is not as straightforward as it seems. Here, seven entrepreneurs give their greatest techniques for mastering the art of small conversation as a business professional.

The beautiful thing about small chat is that you can practically speak about anything, and one of the things most people prefer to discuss is the daily news, Honest Paws co-founder Chelsea Rivera explains.

"Dedicating a portion of your day to learning what is going on in the world minimizes self-doubt in discussions with new individuals," Rivera argues. To do this, corporate executives should subscribe to relevant news providers that give rapid readings of what is happening across the globe every day.

"I started with a major small-talk edge — my dad is Italian," explains Propaganda Premium E-Liquid co-founder Nicholas Denuccio, revealing that as an entrepreneur, this hereditary skill comes in extremely helpful when it comes to interacting effectively with people.

"Ask more questions than you answer. Whether dealing with mentors, suppliers, or consumers, ask a lot of interesting (not nosy) questions. You'll learn a lot," Denuccio advises. As an extra plus, when you ask them about themselves, they will believe you are the finest conversationalist alive, he explains.

Common Giant creator Phillip Oakley agrees: "People prefer to speak about themselves." Entrepreneurs may exploit this truth to enhance their small conversation abilities, and one way to do this is by noting something distinctive about the other person and asking them about it.

Do they use a cool phone case? Are they wearing shoes with formal pants? Do they have intriguing tattoos? These are just a few examples of subjects that might act as discussion starters. "Often, you can get them to open up about their passions, and discover something relevant," Oakley says.

No matter what technique you use, the goal is to make it authentic, according to Craft Impact co-founder and CEO Traci Beach. "Make a point to repeat the other person's name back to them. This helps disarm people and develop rapport, therefore it's crucial to remember someone's name, and to use it throughout a discussion," she suggests.

In addition to repeating their name, it's crucial to question the other person about themselves as a method to engage them more and keep the discussion continuing. "Expressing real attention and interest helps develop relationships of trust," Beach argues.

"Little conversation is 'small' because it is emotionally neutral dialogue without actual depth on noncontroversial issues," argues Justin Faerman, co-founder of Conscious Lifestyle Magazine.

But that doesn't mean it should remain that way — according to Faerman, you can put in emotional depth without touching on sensitive themes, which converts casual chat into very deep, honest, and meaningful interactions. "To achieve this, ask questions like 'What do you enjoy about [the issue at hand]?' and watch the magic unfold."

The art of small talk is not just about speaking, but also about learning how to be comfortable with pauses in conversation, argues WPBeginner co-founder Syed Balkhi.

"It's pretty typical for a small chat to fade down, resulting in an 'awkward' break in discussion. However, pauses don't have to be uncomfortable," Balkhi argues. "It's OK to allow a second or two of quiet to pass by and to contemplate rather than fill it up with words. Be comfortable with quiet and start a new subject after you've had time to consider."

"I come from a society where the small conversation is not a thing," says Karl Kangur, founder and CEO of Above House, adding that no matter how often he rehearsed at conferences, it never seemed authentic.

But the only way to overcome this impediment is to practice more, which is why Kangur's coach recommended he have more random contacts with individuals in his everyday life, from the building security to the barista or the electrician. "This not only revolutionized my interactions in business and at conferences but also opened up many new avenues in my personal life," he continues.

Trick you need to master small talk
It's not simple to initiate a small talk discussion. You need bravery to make the initial move and to do so in a manner that elicits a response. You want to be nice, demonstrate you are open to talk and make a remark that starts the ball going. And there is always the chance that the other person would not reciprocate, but without attempting, you will never know that.
That's why it's so crucial to have some tactics on your sleeve to boost the possibilities of small chat leading to more significant talks. And one of the most fundamental tactics is fairly simple: it's understanding how to word the questions you ask.

Take, for example, the basic dialogue of asking a coworker about his vacation. This may happen in the break room at work, before a meeting, or while dropping by someone's office to say hello. We typically don't pay great attention to how we frame queries we ask. But, small variations in language may have a surprisingly huge influence on the way that discussions evolve.
So, here are two possibilities; see which you believe would be most effective.
Option one is: "Did you have a pleasant vacation?"

And option two is: "How was your vacation?"
Which version do you think would be most likely to lead to a more interesting discussion with your colleague?

If you answered number two, you would be accurate. The reason is that the first question – "Did you have a pleasant vacation?" – is what language specialists would term a "close-ended inquiry" – a question that encourages a straightforward yes or no response. By asking "Did you have a pleasant vacation?" you are letting – even encouraging – your colleague to react with a simple "Yes" or "No" – answering your question, but putting the discussion to rest. For example:
You: Hi Charles, did you appreciate your vacation?
Charles: Yes - that was excellent. Thanks. (and end of chat)

A better alternative for prolonging talks is to employ what language specialists would term an "open-ended question," which was the second variation ("How was your vacation?"). This style of inquiry elicits a more complex answer, which opens options for furthering the discourse naturally. For example:
You: I Charles. How was your vacation?
Charles: It was fantastic. We traveled to Paris for a few days, and then leased a vehicle to drive to the Loire Valley where we rented bikes...
At this point, you have many paths for extending the conversation: Perhaps you've been to France, or are interested in traveling to France. Or maybe you've heard of the Loire Valley but would want to know more.

The idea is that by wording the question in an open-ended approach, you're likely to obtain more information back – which then raises the possibility of a deeper and more interesting discussion with your colleague.

Chapter 4 Becoming a better listener when talking to people and to interact with new people.

Listening is an incredibly necessary talent, tragically undertaught, and physically and psychologically hard. In the aftermath of...more

It's never been more vital — or more challenging — for leaders to be effective listeners. Job hopping is frequent, and remote employment means we don't receive the nonverbal signs we'd pick up from an in-person encounter. Employers that fail to listen and intelligently react to their people's issues will witness increased turnover. And considering that the biggest rates of turnover are among top achievers who can take customers and projects with them, and the frontline personnel responsible for the customer experience, the danger is evident.

While listening is a talent generally commended, it's seldom, if ever, officially taught as such, outside of training for therapists. A 2015 survey indicated that although 78% of recognized undergraduate business schools include "presenting" as a learning aim, just 11% identified "listening."

Listening properly is the type of ability that comes from not just education but coaching – continual, specific training from someone who understands your unique strengths, limitations, and most crucially, habits. Reading this essay won't convert you become a champion listener any more than reading an article about balance would turn you into Simone Biles. Our objectives are to deepen your awareness of what excellent listening is and give research-backed guidance to improve your listening abilities.

Becoming a Better Listener
A participant in every discussion has two goals: first, to grasp what the other person is speaking (both the overt message and the emotion underlying it) and second, to demonstrate attention, involvement, and compassion to the other person. This second purpose is not "merely" for the sake of compassion, which would be justification enough. If individuals do not feel listened to, they will stop to give information.
This is "active listening." It has three aspects:
Cognitive: Paying attention to all the information, both explicit and implicit, that you are getting from the other person, digesting, and integrating that information
Emotional: Staying calm and sympathetic throughout the talk, especially regulating any emotional responses (annoyance, boredom) you may encounter
Behavioral: Conveying attention and understanding vocally and nonverbally
Getting skilled at active listening is a lifelong effort. However, even little adjustments may make a major impact on your listening efficacy. Here's a "cheat sheet" with nine useful tips:

1. Repeat people's last few words back to them.
If you recall nothing else, remember this small exercise that accomplishes so much. It helps the other person feel listened to, keeps you on course throughout the discussion, and gives a break for both of you to collect ideas or recover from an emotional response.

2. Don't "put it in your own words" unless you need to.
Multiple studies have demonstrated that direct repetition works, even if it may seem odd. Rephrasing what your interlocutor has stated, however, may raise both emotional tension and mental strain on both sides. Use this method just when you need to verify your knowledge — and declare, specifically, "I'm going to put this in my own words to make sure I understand."

3. Offer nonverbal signs that you're listening – but only if it comes effortlessly to you.
Eye contact, attentive posture, nodding, and other nonverbal signs are vital, but it's hard to pay attention to someone's words when you're constantly reminding yourself to establish frequent eye contact. If these types of actions would demand a big habit shift, you may instead, let people know at the outset of a discussion that you're on the non-reactive side, and ask for their patience and understanding.

4. Pay attention to nonverbal clues.
Remember that active listening entails paying attention to both the explicit and implicit information that you're getting in a discussion. Nonverbal signals, such as tone

of voice, facial expression, and body language, are generally where the motive and emotion behind the words are communicated.

5. Ask more questions than you believe you need to.
This both enhances the other person's experience of feeling listened to, ensuring that you completely comprehend their message, and may act as a nudge to make sure key information isn't ignored.

6. Minimize distractions as much as possible.
You'll want to avoid noise, interruptions, and other external distractions, but it's crucial to reduce your internal distractions as well. If you are engrossed with another issue, take time to re-center. If you know a talk can be stressful, calm yourself as much as possible before walking in.

7. Acknowledge weaknesses.
If you know going into a conversation that you may be a substandard listener — whether you're weary from a dozen heated talks earlier that day, unfamiliar with the subject under discussion, or any other reason — let the other person know straight away. If you lose your footing during the discussion — a loss of concentration or understanding – explain you didn't quite grasp it, and ask the individual to repeat themselves.

8. Don't practice your answer while the other person is talking.

Take a small pause after they finish speaking to formulate your remarks. This will demand intentional effort! People think roughly four times quicker than other people speak, so you've got spare brainpower when you're a listener. Use it to remain focused and take in as much information as possible.

9. Monitor your emotions.

If you have an emotional response, decelerate the speed of the talk. Do additional repetition, and pay attention to your breathing. You don't want to answer in a manner that will lead the other person to detach. Nor — and this is a subtler thing to avoid — do you want to fall into the simple defensive mechanism of just shutting out what you don't want to hear, or rushing to discredit or argue it away?

The Skills Involved in Active Listening

Listening is a complicated job, with many distinct subtasks, and it's conceivable to be excellent at some and awful at others. Rather than thinking of oneself as a "good listener" or a "bad listener," it might be advantageous to judge yourself on the subskills of active listening. Below is a breakdown of these subskills along with ideas for what to do if you're struggling with any one of them.

First, let's start with what we call the "picking-up abilities," the talents that enable you to obtain the information you need.

1. Hearing

If you have hearing loss, be honest about it. For some reason, individuals would gloat about their bad eyesight yet conceal hearing loss. Help break that stigma. Ask for what you need — e.g., for others to face you while talking, or offer you written materials in advance. Let others know so that they will be attentive to indicators that you may have overlooked anything.

2. Auditory processing
This relates to how effectively the brain makes sense of the acoustic signals. If you're struggling to comprehend someone, ask questions to clarify. If it's beneficial, from time to time reiterate your knowledge of both the issue and the other person's rationale for bringing it up — and ask them to verify or improve it. (Make it obvious that you are doing this for your comprehension.)

3. Reading body language, tone of voice, or social indicators appropriately
The suggestion for auditory processing applies here. Asking a trusted colleague to be your nonverbal communication translator may be beneficial in instances when correct listening is critical, but confidentiality is not.

The following two skills require being mentally present in the conversational moment.

4. Maintaining attention
If you regularly find yourself distracted while attempting to listen to someone, regulate your surroundings as much as possible. Before you begin, create an intention by spending a minute to consciously concentrate on this

person, at this moment, in a discussion that will be about this issue. If applicable, utilize a written agenda or in-the-moment whiteboarding to keep yourself and the other person aligned. If you do have a loss of attention, confess it, apologize, and ask the individual to repeat what they said. (Yes, it's humiliating, but it occurs to everyone periodically and some of us often.) Arrive a few minutes early to adapt yourself if you are having a meeting in a strange environment.

5. Regulating your emotional reaction
Meditation offers both immediate and short-term effects for relaxation and emotional regulation, independent of the specific technique. The idea is to practice it twice a day for 10 to 20 minutes, concentrating on a mental picture or repeating a phrase and eliminating other thoughts as they arise.

At the moment, focus on your breathing and undertake a "grounding exercise" if you feel anxious. These are basic psychological methods that help to attract individuals back to the present moment by focusing attention on the local surroundings. Typical exercises include naming five colored objects that you can see (e.g., green couch, black dog, gold lamp, white door, red rug) or identifying four things that you are hearing, seeing, feeling, and smelling (e.g., hearing birdsong, seeing a chair, feeling chenille upholstery, smelling neighbors' cooking).
Finally, the active listener needs to pull the full package — hearing the message and recognizing its reception — together, in the present. It may be tough!

6. Integrating numerous sources of knowledge.

At the very least, you are both listening to speech and monitoring body language. You may also be listening to many individuals at once, speaking on different platforms concurrently, or listening while also taking in visual information, such as construction designs or sales estimates. Figure out what helps you listen best. Do you require information in advance? A "processing break"? An opportunity to loop back and check everyone's understanding? This is another case where it might be advantageous to have another person taking in the same information, who can fill you in on what you might have missed.

7. "Performing" active listening (e.g., eye contact, nodding, appropriate facial expressions) (e.g., eye contact, nodding, appropriate facial expressions).

If you have a natural poker face or find it easier to pay attention to people's words if you don't establish eye contact, share that information with your discussion partner, and thank them for accommodating you. Do more repetition to make up for the absence of nonverbal communication. You may desire to develop stronger performativity skills, but don't bring that mental strain to critical interactions. Ask a five-year-old to tell you about their favorite superhero, then try acting like you're listening.

Please note: This list is not meant to be a diagnostic tool, but if any of the abilities described above seem particularly challenging to you, you may wish to contact your doctor. Scientific knowledge of these processes, from the sensory organs to the brain, has developed substantially in the last few years. Many successful individuals have realized mid-career that they had undetected sensory, attention, information-processing, or other issues that may impede listening abilities.

For each of these subskills, there is also a spectrum of innate aptitude, and your life experience may have heightened or dampened this potential. We know, for example, that music training increases auditory processing abilities, and acting or improvisation training improves your ability to "read" people and fulfill the role of an engaged listener. Having authority, by contrast, diminishes your capacity to read people and effectively absorb their message - don't allow this to happen to you!

Listening is very essential, woefully undertaught, physically and intellectually hard, and in the aftermath of Covid-19 has never been more difficult. As we close in on the third year of unparalleled change in work and life, workers and managers alike have more questions than ever – worries that they may find it difficult to verbalize for several reasons, from mental fog to the sheer novelty of the issue.

When this occurs, take a minute to listen intently. Consider the questioner, not merely the question. Now is the moment for leaders to genuinely listen, comprehend the context, avoid the desire to reply with generic solutions, acknowledge their listening limits – and improve on them. Have compassion for yourself – you can't shout at your brain like a drill sergeant and whip that raw grey matter into shape. What you can do is identify your weak spots and make the required improvements.

Listening is also challenging because we're frequently concerned with ourselves, says Hal Gregersen, executive director of the MIT Leadership Center. "It's incredibly hard to enter into a discussion without my agenda being emblazoned on my forehead and your agenda writing on yours," he adds. "Unfortunately with the frantic, chaotic, difficult pace of professional life nowadays, individuals are even more determined to get their agenda accomplished."

WHY LISTENING IS CRITICAL
When you start a discussion thinking exclusively of your agenda, your objective is to maneuver and manage the conversation and to come out better than the other person, says Gregersen.
"I may encourage you to do, purchase, or act, but the possibility that I acquire any significantly new data is close to zero," he adds. "I'm thinking that the dialogue is about me, or it's about me dominating you. Neither are fantastic discussion starters."
Walking about with closed ears is OK if what you're doing is the correct thing and the world doesn't change. "But if the world changes and we happen to not be doing the correct thing, it becomes vital to pay attention to other people's ideas, emotions, words, sentiments, and perspectives," adds Gregersen. "It's crucial to be open to

fresh information that you're not seeking but need to hear."

How do you break harmful habits? Here are six techniques to become a better listener:

1. LISTEN TO LEARN, NOT BE POLITE

"Often, whether recognizing it or not, people listen to one other out of charity, not out of curiosity," says Ajit Singh, partner for the early-stage startup fund Artiman Ventures and consulting professor in the School of Medicine at Stanford University. "Listening is excellent, but the objective needs to be inquiry, not kindness. True conversation can not happen when we pretend to listen, and it surely cannot happen if we are not listening at all."

"If we ever leave a discussion and learned nothing remarkable, we weren't truly listening."

"Each day, ask yourself, 'What am I going to be fascinated about?'" adds Gregersen. "Stewart Brand, [editor of the Whole Earth Catalog,] wakes up every day asking himself, 'How many things am I dead wrong about?' Both inquiries successfully open your ears. It's having a beginner's mindset entering into a conversation."

2. QUIET YOUR AGENDA

While you can't control someone else's listening habits, you can manage your own, and that requires quieting down your thoughts.

"Turn off those agendas," urges Gregersen. "Listen to what someone else is trying to convey. We need

51

disconfirming information, not confirming. If we ever conclude a discussion and learned nothing remarkable, we weren't truly listening."

3. ASK MORE QUESTIONS
One of the easiest ways to be a better listener is to ask more questions than you provide answers, says Gregersen. When you ask questions, you create a safe environment for other people to tell you an unvarnished truth.

"Listening with true focus means I'm going to be open to being incorrect, and I'm fine with that in this conversation," adds Gregersen. "In a world that's increasingly more politicized, being able to listen is crucial to eliminating avoidable conflict at any level, inside a team, company, or on a bigger political nation level," he adds.

4. PAY ATTENTION TO YOUR TALK/LISTEN TO RATIO
Strive for a 2:1 ratio of listening to talking, urges Eblin. "If you're a note taker during meetings or talks, consider keeping track of how much you listen vs how much you talk," he advises. "Mark out an area of the paper and write down the names of all the persons on the conference call. Whenever a person speaks for more than a phrase or two, add a check mark beside his or her name. That includes you, too. The visual representation of comparing listening to talking might hold some lessons for you."

5. REPEAT BACK WHAT YOU HEARD

Some problems interfere with people's ability to understand accurately what another person is trying to communicate, says Adam Goodman, director of the Center for Leadership at Northwestern University. "Am I anticipating what the other person is about to say? Do I agree or disagree with what's being said? Maybe I'm agreeing too soon and, upon contemplation, I'd find myself disagreeing later?" he says. "Put simply, there's more potential to misinterpret than there is to genuinely understand."

Instead, employ a mechanism called active listening. "It's been around for a long time, and works if done right," adds Goodman. The primary notion is repeating back to the speaker what you heard. If the speaker agrees that what you heard is what he or she meant to say, you may continue. If not, the speaker has to restate their point until the audience does comprehend.

6. WAIT UNTIL SOMEONE IS DONE TALKING BEFORE YOU RESPOND

The most challenging component of listening successfully is waiting for a period after a phrase before developing a reply, says Leslie Shore, author of Listen to Succeed.

"When we begin working on a reply before the speaker is through, we miss both the whole information being delivered and a comprehension of the sort of emotion present in the speaker's delivery," she says in her book.

This is risky, warns Gregersen. "When I'm the most important thing in the world, that's the time when I'm most likely to be thinking about the next thing I'm going to say instead of listening to you," he adds. "At the very heart, that's what going on; I'm proclaiming to the world I am more important than you. That's an unpleasant moment of self-awareness, and a self-serving manner of approaching life."
We all need self-focus, but leaders who make a difference are the ones who recognize the mission is broader than themselves, says Gregersen. "When a leader is functioning on the border of what's feasible, they're in strong listening mode," he adds.

Interacting with new individuals
1. Identify your reluctance. Why aren't you communicating with people now? Are you engaging with others yet feel like you're doing it wrong? If you can identify the issue, it will go a long way toward helping you overcome it. In the meanwhile, try the advice below.
2. Overcome your social nervousness. For many individuals, engaging with others is unpleasant, yet avoidance is not an effective option. [2] If you become scared about talking to others, you may want to concentrate on managing your nervousness first.
3. Believe in yourself. If you are frightened that you will fail to establish friends, or that you will continuously offend people, you're going to have a very hard time communicating with others. Believe in yourself and you will find interactions growing simpler and easier.

4. Build your self-esteem. If you spend a chunk of time believing that no one will want to chat with you because they're so much better than you are, you'll lose out on a fantastic world of interaction! Spend some time realizing how amazing you are and you'll see the world in a different light.

5. Be confident. Lack of self-confidence may make it incredibly hard to engage with others, frequently because others perceive that you are not confident and that makes them anxious. Build your self-confidence or at least learn how to fake it to make people like you more.

6. Practice. As with any talent (and social interaction is a skill), you can grow better at it by practicing. Practice your social skills by utilizing them as often as possible. You may start by connecting with family members or even simply strangers that you see, such as grocers and bank workers.

Starting Interactions

1. Introduce yourself. When interacting with someone for the first time, it's a good idea to introduce yourself. Where in the conversation you introduce yourself, however, will depend on the individual conversation.

Walking up to a stranger and introducing yourself before saying anything else makes it appear like you're selling something (or simply crazy) (or just weird).

Introducing oneself when you first meet someone at a party, though, is a smart idea. Especially if it's an official gathering, like a company party.

2. Talk to strangers. If you're not engaging with people much now but you'd want to start, chances are you're going to have to chat with some strangers. It's not as horrible as it sounds! Find a cause to speak out and simply let things flow organically. Who knows: maybe you'll meet a new buddy!

If you're trying to start a conversation with your crush, you might ask a question, compliment them, or say something genuine.

3. Make friends. The finest individuals to engage with our friends and having more of them will only enhance your life. For those who are timid or not particularly sociable, though, finding friends might seem incredibly hard. But with some work and patience, you can create plenty of friends. Just remember to be yourself and only maintain pals in your life that make you a better person!

4. Treat your friends nicely. As for the friends you have, treat those pals properly. This will assist with many encounters. Help folks who are having a hard time by communicating with them. Listen to them when they give you a tale about their day. You get the idea.

5. Talk with your buddies. Even when you feel like you don't have much to speak about, you should strive to initiate discussions. Awkward silences might lead your pals to worry or grow nervous...even make them feel forgotten!

6. Make your talks amazing. Make the discussions that you do have excellent ones. Ask questions, truly listen, and take an active position in the discourse. Don't

dominate the discussion time and don't be too silent either.

Creating Opportunity

1. Take advantage of your peers. Whether you're a student or an adult, you should have individuals in your life whom you can engage with: peers. Your classmates or employees make terrific folks to engage with.
2. Join an online community. Especially for persons with a lot of social anxiety, online groups may be an excellent place to practice social interaction. You may join a fan club for a TV program or book you enjoy or you can volunteer with sites like wikiHow!
3. Join a local club. There are real-life clubs and organizations as well. These are much better for practicing your social interactions. Most schools will offer a range of clubs, but adults may also discover groups (typically via a local library or community center) (often through a local library or community center).
4. Volunteer. Volunteering is a terrific way to meet people and also give back to your community at the same time. From soup kitchens to fundraisers, constructing houses to sheltering animals, there are many ways to assist your community and you'll have the opportunity to meet individuals with similar ideals!
5. Join a religious organization. Whether it's a church, temple, or other religious organization, these institutions may offer a secure setting in which to meet people and connect, establishing new friends with similar interests and beliefs. There is a group for almost any belief system, so give it a try.

6. Be more social with existing friends. If you don't like the sounds of these, you can always simply be more sociable with the people you have. Try to have a quiet party or join a book club. Whatever sounds nice to you and is entertaining for your buddies!

Interacting Well
1. Be kind. Be nice when you talk to other people. Acknowledge them and be positive in your interactions. Don't lie or talk about them behind their backs. Treat them the way that you would like to be treated!
2. Be nice. Be nice when you chat with others. Importantly, be nice to everyone. Always. Even when they're disrespectful to you. Say words like "please" and "thank you", and let them complete speaking before you start talking. You should also be patient with them. Just as you have a hard time dealing with others, they could too (or perhaps have additional challenges, like disabilities or mental illness) (or even have other problems, like disability or mental illness). Act in a manner that would make your grandma pleased and you should be set.
3. Be humble. When you talk with people, be humble. Don't brag or spend a bunch of time talking about yourself. This causes people, not like you and not want to communicate with you anymore. Allow everyone to say and don't attempt to one-up them when they tell you anything.
4. Be friendly. Be nice when you chat with others. Don't look indifferent or that you don't care about them. Keep

eye contact, smile, listen, and reflect a cheerful attitude (even if you're in a negative one).

5. Be courteous. Be polite to everyone you contact with. Allow them to communicate, don't say or do anything disrespectful, appreciate their differences, and generally treat them the way that you would like to be treated.

6. Listen. The most crucial component of engaging properly with people is to listen to them. It's a lot less about how much you say or how you say it, and more down to how you react to the things that you genuinely hear them say. Practice your fundamental listening skills, as well as your ability to read between the lines, and you'll be communicating like a pro in no time!

Printed in Great Britain
by Amazon